Activities We Do

We Make Music

by Connor Stratton

FOCUS READERS
SCOUT

www.focusreaders.com

Focus Readers is distributed by North Star Editions:
sales@northstareditions.com | 888-417-0195

Produced for Focus Readers by Red Line Editorial.

Photographs ©: wavebreakmedia/Shutterstock Images, cover, 1; PR Image Factory/ Shutterstock Images, 4; Aimstock/iStockphoto, 7; fotostorm/iStockphoto, 9 (top); Hruan/ iStockphoto, 9 (bottom); SolStock/iStockphoto, 11; Africa Studio/Shutterstock Images, 13 (top), 16 (top right); Daisy Daisy/Shutterstock Images, 13 (bottom); FatCamera/ iStockphoto, 15; tarasov_vl/iStockphoto, 16 (top left); tusumaru/iStockphoto, 16 (bottom left); EasyBuy4u/iStockphoto, 16 (bottom right)

Library of Congress Cataloging-in-Publication Data
Names: Stratton, Connor, author.
Title: We make music / by Connor Stratton.
Description: Lake Elmo, MN : Focus Readers, 2020. | Series: Activities we do | Audience: K to Grade 3. | Includes index.
Identifiers: LCCN 2019002982 (print) | LCCN 2019003553 (ebook) | ISBN 9781641859967 (pdf) | ISBN 9781641859394 (ebook) | ISBN 9781641858014 (hardcover) | ISBN 9781641858700 (pbk.)
Subjects: LCSH: Music--Performance--Juvenile literature.
Classification: LCC ML457 (ebook) | LCC ML457 .S8 2020 (print) | DDC 781.4/3--dc23
LC record available at https://lccn.loc.gov/2019002982

Printed in the United States of America
Mankato, MN
May, 2019

About the Author

Connor Stratton loves playing the saxophone, eating popcorn, and watching movies with friends. He lives in Minnesota.

Table of Contents

Music Is Fun

We love to make music.

We make sounds.

We hear what we play.

We can sing.

We can clap.

We can play instruments.

clap
instrument

Instruments

Each instrument is different.

We play the **guitar**.

We play the **drum**.

We play the **piano**.

guitar
drum

piano

We play our instruments together.
We play a song.

Practice

We practice making music.

We learn the **notes**.

Our teacher helps us.

notes

We learn a new song.

The song is hard to play.

Practice makes it easier.

Glossary

drum

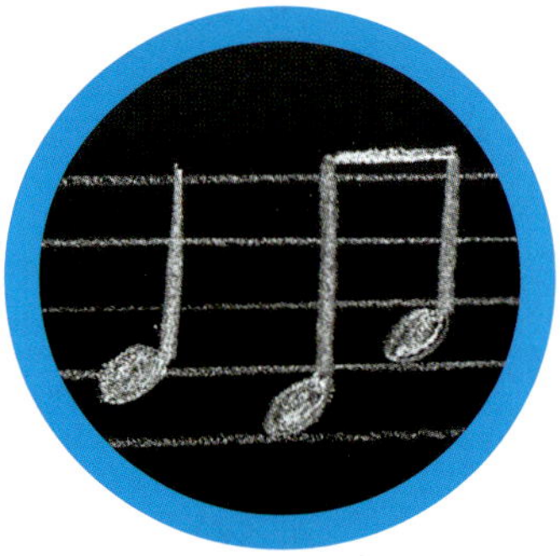

notes

guitar

piano

Index